Created for you:

The Surviving Bullies Project

"There is love in this book and plenty of useful advice born from the hardscrabble experience of once being there..."

~ Charles Laird Calia, father of two daughters
Author of *The Unspeakable* and *The Stargazing Year*

SURVIVING BULLIES WORKBOOK

The **Surviving Bullies Project** is a grassroots effort dedicated to helping targets of bullying. The SBP strives to provide practical resources for the targets of bullying. It is also dedicated to empowering the targets, bullies, and bystanders to improve the social climate for all.

ISBN: 1-4116-7649-1

Learn more about the Surviving Bullies Project on the web at www.survivingbullies.com

Written by Dickon Pownall-Gray

Illustrated by Shan Shan Jiang

Mistakes do occasionally occur despite conscientious effort to ensure this workbook is complete and error free. If you find an error, please let us know by emailing errors@survivingbullies.com. Corrections will be implemented in subsequent editions.

SURVIVING BULLIES WORKBOOK

REVIEWS

Reviews from Our Readers

From Hadar Lubin, M.D., mother, Co-Director of Post Traumatic Stress Center in New Haven, Connecticut, and Assistant Clinical Professor at Yale University School of Medicine

"The *Surviving Bullies Workbook* is an essential, empowering, and effective tool to have in the journey of overcoming the devastating effects of bullying. It guides the readers, step-by-step, in how to disentangle themselves from the web of shame and humiliation cast by the bully."

From Jocelyn Shur, age 16, recovering target of bullying and aspiring writer, plans to pursue a major in psychology

"This challenging workbook is an empowering guide that I wish I could have had access to when I was experiencing being bullied. I think it is an unique and an effective tool that will absolutely help any victim...By using this resource one will develop a greater understanding of his or her situation and thus handle conflict in a more sophisticated and confident manner. The workbook is very personalized and it is obvious that the questions are created by someone with real experiences; therefore the insight is extremely accurate, and although personal it is universal..."

From Charles Laird Calia, father of two daughters and author

"A guide not just for teens but also for their parents, *Surviving Bullies Workbook* condenses the often frightful lessons of growing up in just a few simple words: You are not alone. There is love in this book and plenty of useful advice born from the hardscrabble experience of once being there, experience that makes the *Surviving Bullies Workbook* an essential handbook for every child, parent, and educator facing the awful vicissitudes of life."

From Scott Brown, father of four and author of How to Negotiate with Kids

"This is an innovative approach to an important problem - the most practical antidote to bullying I have found."

From Debra Lynn Mucha, mother and recovering target of bullying

"When I was 13 years old, my parents took me to see a therapist because I was unhappy. I could not articulate why I felt this way. The therapist diagnosed me as having 'normal' teenage girl issues. If the therapist had a copy of this book, it would have aided me in expressing my thoughts and feelings. Maybe I could have had appropriate counseling at age 14 instead of age 54."

Reviews from Our Readers (cont.)

From Tracy Pennoyer, Ph.D., mother and school psychologist

"In a direct and open way, this workbook compassionately addresses the pain of being bullied while giving kids active support and tools to enable them to take charge of their lives. The reader will feel that the authors stand with them through this difficult process."

From Ron Baglio, father and Deputy Headmaster, The Eagle Hill School in Massachusetts

"Dickon Pownall-Gray is a caring person and an excellent listener. The *Surviving Bullies Workbook* is the result of countless hours of interviews with the individuals who need this book the most - kids. The only actions you can control are your own. This book is a tool that will allow a victim of bullying to take back that control and move forward in a proud and purposeful manner. When a child feels empowered, success is right around the corner."

From Gabrielle de Wardener, mother and Human Resources Director, Loyalty Management Group

"Bullying is as insidious in the workplace as it is in the classroom. This thoughtful workbook provides a comprehensive set of tools to equip victims of bullying to muster their inner resources, fully understand their situation and move out of their isolation. The step-by-step format is clear, the tone sympathetic, the direction action-focused."

From Robyn Altman, LMSW, mother and clinical social worker

"As both a social worker and mother, I find this workbook to be a valuable tool for those who feel alone and isolated. The workbook teaches bullied individuals empowerment and how "Not" to be a victim. Building self-esteem and awareness of self is essential during the vulnerable years of childhood and adolescence."

From Andrew Pownall-Gray, father and aspiring race car driver

"The victim of bullying may be desperate for a way forward or resigned to accept their position. In either case, the workbook will encourage a desire for change. If my brother, Dickon, had this workbook at the age of 11, it could have greatly improved his life at that time."

Reviews from Our Readers (cont.)

From Beau Doherty, father, President of Special Olympics Connecticut, and former target of bullying

"In my young life, I moved from Massachusetts to Minnesota where a Boston accent and an Irish heritage were viewed as different. I was bullied and went through all the various emotions including rage which landed me a suspension from school. My experiences in my youth have sensitized me to the population I have served for 30 years. I found the *Surviving Bullies Workbook* to have realistic skills that help bullied people cope, take control of their situation and understand the mind-set of a bully. I find that these interventions help one to free themselves from the haunting feeling that there is something wrong with them."

From Mark Valenzia, father and CEO, The Dormy House Companies

"The *Surviving Bullies Workbook* is written in simple language that does not come across as patronizing and is easily readable. The workbook is informative, which will assist with the reader's understanding of their enigma. Above all, if the recommended tasks are undertaken as suggested, I have no doubt that the subject will be able to forge a way through their perceived hopelessness."

From Christopher Henrich, Ph.D., Assistant Professor, Department of Psychology, Georgia State University

"The *Surviving Bullies Workbook* is an impressive toolkit of skills to help teens better cope with being bullied. The workbook succeeds in translating psychological research and theory pertinent to bullying into straightforward language that should resonate with teens. This workbook will be a valuable asset for victims of bullying who are striving to take back control of their lives from the bullies."

From Ben Fine, age 16, high school junior, lacrosse player and National Merit Scholar

"Dickon Pownall-Gray's *Surviving Bullies Workbook* offers a critically needed comprehensive system for dealing with bullies in a highly user-friendly workbook. This insightful workbook helps kids develop the skills to interact more comfortably and gain acceptance. It should be a mandatory read for all students, regardless of whether they have been bullied because it imparts tactics useful for life."

Reviews from Our Readers (cont.)

From Brenda and Keith Bedingham, co-founders of Verax International

"The *Surviving Bullies Workbook* provides a simple to use, practical framework for a bullied child or adult to follow -- although mainly aimed at children. It is written by people who have a real understanding of what it means to be bullied -- a result of their own experiences as children."

From Katie Noonan, Ph.D., mother and organizational psychologist

"It is widely known that lack of control is one of the greatest causes of stress. This straightforward guide, through its insights, "secret agent" interactive format, and actionable advice, returns some control to kids rendered helpless and hopeless by bullies - giving them a powerful and much needed emotional boost. What a gift!"

From Rev. Jennifer Brooks, J.D., The Unitarian Universalist Church on Nantucket Island and mother

"The *Surviving Bullies Workbook* is a remarkable resource for children. It guides and empowers - successfully combining frank talk with a light touch. Copies of the workbook should be strewn about, free for the taking, everywhere children congregate. A 'must read' for teachers, youth advisors, and clergy."

From Jerry Friedman, father and professional fashion photographer

"The *Surviving Bullies Workbook* is a courageous effort to confront one of childhood's most unspoken, widespread traumas. Bullying, like many diseases, can rob a child of his or her potential. This workbook gives the child and the parent a positive approach and systematic framework to tackle the problem and overcome it."

From Daniel Bendor, M.D., Assistant Clinical Professor Dept. of Psychiatry, Yale University School of Medicine and staff psychiatrist, Child and Family Agency of South-Eastern Connecticut

"This is an outstandingly clear and practical manual... Because it is so useful, it belongs in the offices of private therapists, clinics, and school personnel. I can only hope the authors are working on a similar manual for primary school students."

SURVIVING BULLIES WORKBOOK

"No one can make you feel inferior without your consent."
~ Eleanor Roosevelt

MISSIONS ROAD MAP

SURVIVING BULLIES WORKBOOK

"No one can make you feel inferior without your consent."
~ Eleanor Roosevelt

Table of Contents

Missions Introduction	**Page ii-viii**
Mission One: Complete Incident Report	**Page 1-16**
Mission Two: Demystify My Bullies	**Page 17-24**
Mission Three: Escape From The Isolation Trap	**Page 25-38**
Mission Four: Develop Your Bully Antidote	**Page 39-56**
Mission Five: Make Friends!	**Page 57-70**
About the Creators: •Anti-Bullying Agent Profiles •Acknowledgments	**Page I-IX**

SURVIVING BULLIES WORKBOOK

"Targets of bullying, you are not alone."
~ Your Mission Control Team

YOUR MISSION CONTROL TEAM

ANTI-BULLYING AGENT: Dickon Pownall-Gray

Age: 51
Mission Assignment: Creator, *Surviving Bullies Workbook*
Bullying Status: Former target [90% recovered]
Profile: From age 11 to 14, I was cruelly bullied. One day, a 17-year-old boy jumped me on my way home from school and beat me up. Finally, he threw me into a barbed wire fence and drove off laughing. The weight of my body forced the rusty steel barbs so deeply into my flesh that I could not untangle myself...Some time later in the emergency room, my mother's demands combined with the doctor's orders made me surrender the boy's name. It was the worst decision of my life...

ANTI-BULLYING AGENT: Shan Shan Jiang

Age: 22
Mission Assignment: Illustrator, *Surviving Bullies Workbook*
Bullying Status: Former target [still recovering]
Profile: After moving to the U.S. at nine years old from China, I stopped fitting in. I was one of four Asian kids in a mostly Italian-American school, and that made my life hellish. Seventh grade was the worst. Besides the "ching chang chung" people constantly muttered at me in the halls, some girls routinely stuck clumps of tape in my hair and watched as I tried to get them out...Seventh grade was when I experienced loneliness from hell. Everywhere I went, I felt like a thorn, awkward, repulsive, and chinky...

Note: Full agent profiles are found in Appendix at the back.

SURVIVING BULLIES WORKBOOK

"No one can make you feel inferior without your consent."
~ Eleanor Roosevelt

MISSIONS BRIEFING

bul·ly·ing, *n.*

A deliberate, repeated or long-term exposure to negative acts performed by a person or a group of persons of higher status or greater strength than the target.[1]

When you are being consistently bullied at school, on the bus, or in your neighborhood, it is emotionally difficult to find the strength to go to school, day after day. Having a plan is the key to overcoming your bullying problem, but the tough question is: what's an effective plan when you are being picked on by four or five boys or girls who may be bigger, older, or seemingly "more popular" than you?

Running away may solve your problems temporarily, but it does not resolve the problems in the long run. Fighting back verbally or physically can work, but it often fails because you are outnumbered and facing opponents who are simply too powerful.

So what can you do if running away solves little and fighting back physically or verbally has only a small chance of success? The answer is: **go through this workbook.**

---

1   Olweus D. *Bullying at school: What we know and what we can do.* Oxford: Blackwell Publishers, 1993.

MISSIONS BRIEFING (continued)

The *Surviving Bullies Workbook* takes you on a set of five missions that will help protect you from being bullied in the future. Here are the missions:

1.   Mission One: Complete Incident Report - to better understand your situation.

2.   Mission Two: Demystify Your Bullies - to understand who your bullies really are as individuals. They are human, after all.

3.   Mission Three: Escape From The Isolation Trap - to figure out how to rebuild your confidence and self-esteem.

4.   Mission Four: Develop Your Bully Antidote - to figure out practical steps that you can take to prevent bullies from picking on you.

5.   Mission Five: Make Friends - to protect yourself from bullies through strengthening friendships and social networks. This is your most important mission.

"No one can make you feel inferior without your consent."
~ Eleanor Roosevelt

MISSIONS
OBJECTIVE

MISSIONS OBJECTIVE:

To move yourself from the bully UNSAFE zone to the bully SAFE zone!

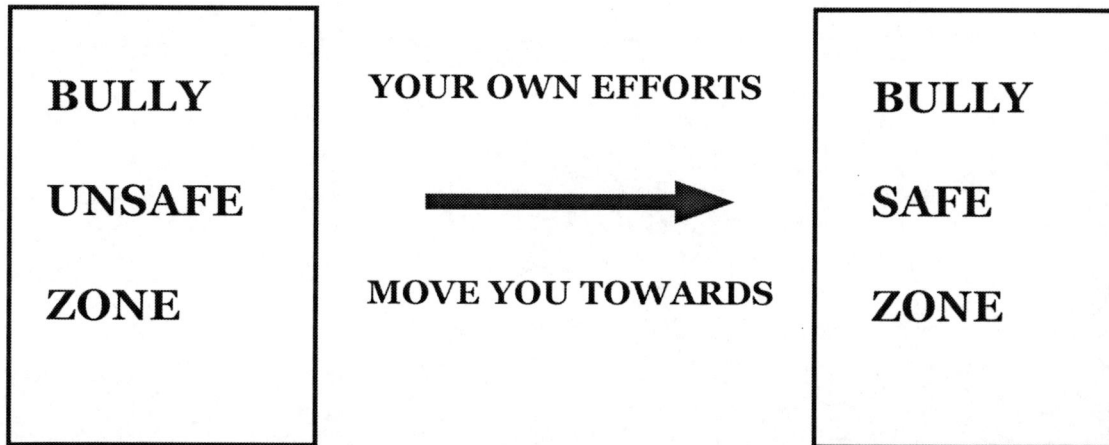

| BULLY UNSAFE ZONE | YOUR OWN EFFORTS → MOVE YOU TOWARDS | BULLY SAFE ZONE |

SURVIVING BULLIES WORKBOOK

PERSONAL

AND

CONFIDENTIAL

Date:

Filled in By:

MISSIONS INSTRUCTIONS

1. This workbook consists of five self-contained missions. We recommend that you complete them in the order provided (Mission 1-5). These are challenging missions. So we suggest that you take a break at the end of each mission. Also keep an open mind and don't feel discouraged if the missions don't go as planned. Remember that the success of each mission is *not* measured by how well you do on the tasks. It is measured by how much you learn from them.

2. Please answer the questions as openly and honestly as you can. They are designed to help you. Remember, this workbook is completely confidential.

3. If you want to work through this workbook on your own without involving any adults, that is fine. But if you find yourself feeling overwhelmed, think about whether you know an adult who might provide support (e.g. your parents, a family friend, a relative, or a person from your church, synagogue, or community). The best person to go to is someone who understands bullying and respects your fear that "ratting" might make your bullying situation worse.

5. For additional copies of the *Surviving Bullies Workbook*, please visit:

www.survivingbullies.com

Note: This workbook is not a quick fix. Your missions will require time and courage. Get ready. Let's begin!

SURVIVING BULLIES WORKBOOK

MISSION ONE:

COMPLETE INCIDENT REPORT

SURVIVING BULLIES WORKBOOK

Completing the Incident Report...

Many individuals who are being bullied describe their experiences as similar to getting lost in a dense fog – a fog where one's emotions become confused, where one can no longer tell a friend from a foe, and even bystanders seem to have turned hostile.

Suddenly, buildings that were once safe have morphed into menacing corridors where bullies may lurk. School buses have now become confined spaces with no escape. The formerly innocent comments of classmates now seem to take on malicious double meanings.

The purpose of the Incident Report is to help you cut through the fog of confusion caused by you being bullied.

The process of recording the facts will allow you to think clearly and objectively about what is happening to you.

Specifically, the Incident Report has been designed to help you work out:

- **Who** is bullying you?
- **Where** are they bullying you?
- **How** are they bullying you?
- **How severely** are they bullying you?

Please continue to the next page.

SURVIVING BULLIES WORKBOOK

Completing the Incident Report...(continued)

Most importantly, this section will help you accurately record the complex feelings you have about being bullied. Please fill out the Incident Report based on your most typical experience with bullying. If you are being bullied in a number of ways, please make note of this in the comments sections.

Remember, your goal is to accurately report how you are being bullied. By doing so, you will be able to move forward and solve your bullying problem based on real facts, not on confusion. Once again, this workbook is confidential. So please answer the questions as openly and honestly as you can. Lets begin!

SURVIVING BULLIES WORKBOOK

Basic Facts

Date of Incident(s):   Day / Month / Year

? ? 14/15

Time of Incident(s):

How many bullies were involved?

(1?) 2? 3? 4? 5?   Or more?

Names of Bullies:

	Nickname	First Name	Last Name
1.		Aaron	
2.			
3.			
4.			
5.			
6.			

Do you think the bullying was:

Verbal?   (Yes)   No

Physical?   Yes   (No)

Racial?   Yes   (No)

Sexual?   Yes   (No)

Other: (describe briefly below)

_____

_____

_____

_____

Basic Facts (cont.)

Where exactly did the bullying take place?

Home or near home?	Yes	No
Traveling to school?	Yes	No
On a school bus?	Yes	No
At school?	*Yes*	No

Place an "X" on the map to show where the incident(s) took place:

If this map does not look like your school, go to the next page and draw a map of your school.
Or if the incident(s) took place outside of your school, go to the next page and draw a map
showing where you were bullied. Then mark an "X" on the spot(s) where your bullying
incident(s) took place.

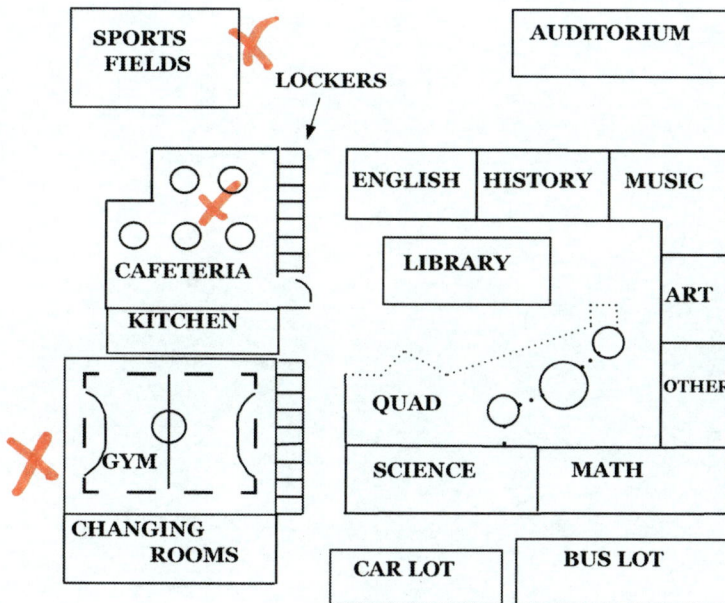

front off school

Use the space provided below and on the following page to draw your own map(s) of where you were bullied.

SURVIVING BULLIES WORKBOOK

INCIDENT REPORT

Basic Facts (cont.)

Comments:

SURVIVING BULLIES WORKBOOK

Was it Physical?

Was the bullying incident(s) physical in nature?   YES   NO

If YES, circle the description of the incident(s) that most closely describes what you experienced. Then, carefully describe what happened to you in the space provided below. If your incident(s) was not physical in nature, skip this page and go to the next humiliation section (i.e. verbal, racial or sexual humiliation).

PHYSICAL HUMILIATION

LESS SEVERE ◀ – – – – – – – ▶ **SEVERE**

• Jostling with shoulders	• Writing in target's schoolbooks	• Kicking with feet	• Threatening with a weapon
• Pushing with hands	• Stealing target's property	• Punching with fists	• Locking in a dark place
• Shoving into others	• Stealing target's homework	• Spitting, scratching, biting, pulling target's hair	• Inflicting lasting physical harm
• Elbowing when passing		• Pulling off target's pants in front of peers	• Physical assault on target's family or friends

---

Please write down exactly what happened to you:

Please continue to the next page.

SURVIVING BULLIES WORKBOOK

Was it Physical? (cont.)

Please write down below more details about the physical bullying that you have been experiencing.

Be sure to answer: How many times a month are you being physically humiliated? Is it the same kind of physical humiliation each time or does it vary? Is it just one bully who is doing this or is it a group of bullies? Does the group have a leader or does the group leader often change?

SURVIVING BULLIES WORKBOOK

Was it Verbal?

Was the bullying incident(s) verbal in nature?   YES   NO

If YES, circle the descriptions of the incident(s) that most closely describes what you experienced. On the next page, carefully describe exactly what happened to you.

VERBAL HUMILIATION

LESS SEVERE ← – – – – – – → SEVERE			
• Referring to the target by derogative nicknames • Mocking the target in front of his/her peers • Mocking the target's style of talking • Making the target the "fall guy" of jokes ▸	• Making personal comments about the target's facial features • Making personal comments about the target's physique • Making negative comments about the target's clothing and sense of fashion • Making negative comments about the target's intelligence	• Telling the target that his or her close friends do not like the target anymore • Making intimidating (anonymous) phone calls to the target's home • Threatening to humiliate the target in front of his or her friends if the target will not hand over lunch money, etc.	• Verbal threats of physical harm to target and or his possessions such as clothes, school books, locker items • Verbal threats of physical harm to the target outside of school so as to leave the target with no sanctuary • Verbal threats of physical harm to the target's friends if they continue to be friends with the target

Please continue to the next page.

SURVIVING BULLIES WORKBOOK

INCIDENT REPORT

Was it Verbal? (cont.)

Please write down exactly what happened to you in the space provided below.

Be sure to answer: How many times a month are you being verbally humiliated? Is it the same sort of verbal humiliation each time or does it vary? Is it just one bully who is doing this or is it a group of bullies? Does the group have a leader or does the group leader often change?

Was it Racial?

Was the bullying incident(s) racial in nature?   YES   NO

If YES, circle the description of the incident(s) that most closely describes what you experienced.   If the incident(s) was not racial in nature, skip this page and go to the next section.

RACIAL HUMILIATION

LESS SEVERE ← — — — — — → SEVERE			
• Telling racially biased jokes	• Insulting with a racial bias	• Excluding the target from teams, clubs, or groups based on race	• Destruction of target's property due to race hatred
• Mocking ethnic clothing	• Spreading racially biased rumors about the target	• Coercing the the target to not respect family racial customs, e.g. wearing a turban	• Physical attack on target because of his or her race
• Mocking other country's traditions	• Writing racially derogative graffitti on walls		• Threatening the target's friends in chat rooms and via Instant Messenger with physical harm
• Making fun of foreign accents	• Emailing target racially biased jokes, stories and personal comments	• Systematically demeaning the target's country of origin and its people	

Please continue to the next page.

SURVIVING BULLIES WORKBOOK

Was it Racial? (cont.)

Please write down exactly what happened to you in the space provided below.

Be sure to answer: How many times a month are you being racially humiliated? Is it the same sort of racial humiliation each time or does it vary? Is it just one bully who is doing this or is it a group of bullies? Does the group have a leader or does the group leader often change?

Was it Sexual?

Was the bullying incident(s) sexual in nature?   YES   NO

If YES, circle the description of the incident(s) that most closely describes what you experienced. On the next page, carefully describe exactly what happened to you.

SEXUAL HUMILIATION

LESS SEVERE ← - - - - - - - → **SEVERE**

• Telling sexual jokes within the target's earshot	• Leers, whistles, catcalls	• Creating rumors of the target having had sex with another	• Secretly telling a girl target's male and female peers that the target is crazy for sex and will give oral sex to any boy brave enough to ask for it
• Steering conversation into too personal areas	• Bra snapping	• Grabbing the victim's breasts or butt	
	• Verbal requests for unwanted sex		
• Calling a boy target gay	• Repeatedly asking target to go on unwanted dates	• Crowding the target (standing too close, cornering, following too close, etc.)	• Spreading rumors that a boy target is having sex with another boy
• Calling a girl target a lesbian	• De-panting		
• Undermining a boy target's athletic prowess	• Calling a girl target a slut or a whore	• Systematically suggesting to a boy target's male and female friends that the target lacks virility and is destined to become gay	• Threats of sexual assault
• Undermining a girl target's belief in her beauty			• Sexual assault
			• Rape

Please continue to the next page.

Was it Sexual? (cont.)

Please write down exactly what happened to you in the space provided below.

Be sure to answer: How many times a month are you being sexually humiliated? Is it the same sort of sexual humiliation each time or does it vary? Is it just one bully who is doing this or is it a group of bullies? Does the group have a leader or does the group leader often change? Do the rumors seem to get more exaggerated over time?

SURVIVING BULLIES WORKBOOK

How Did You Feel Afterwards?

Please circle the words that most describe how you felt immediately after the incident(s), then circle a number from 1 to 5 to describe the intensity of your feelings.

For example, if you felt a little ashamed, circle the number 1. If you felt very ashamed, circle the number 5.

Anger	1	2	3	4	5
Fear	1	2	3	4	5
Rage	1	2	3	4	5
Shame	1	2	3	4	5
Humiliation	1	2	3	4	5
Loneliness	1	2	3	4	5
Self-Hatred	1	2	3	4	5
Pathetic	1	2	3	4	5
Hopeless	1	2	3	4	5
Desire for Revenge	1	2	3	4	5

Now, look over your scores. If you find that you're scoring high on this exercise, don't worry. You're entitled to strong feelings because being bullied is a difficult experience. It's very important for you to be mindful of your future actions because strong emotions can lead to impulsive and destructive behavior.

MISSION TWO:

DEMYSTIFY YOUR BULLIES

Demystifying Your Bullies...

Individuals who have been targets of bullying often recall their bullies as "larger than life" - more powerful than they really are. It is crucial to remember that bullies are individuals just like you. Like you, they have strengths and weaknesses, likes and dislikes, and fears and loves.

The goal of the "Demystify Your Bullies" mission is to help you see your bullies as individuals, not as supermen or superwomen. Think like a detective! Your job is to quietly observe your bullies - to find out who they really are. Discover their strengths and weaknesses, their friends, who they are afraid of, and where they like to hang out.

Entering a dark room for the first time can be very frightening. By understanding your bullies, you can make them less frightening, less powerful, like turning on the light in a dark room.

SURVIVING BULLIES WORKBOOK

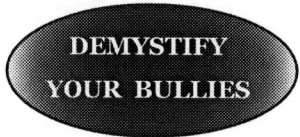

DEMYSTIFY
YOUR BULLIES

The next set of questions is designed to help you better understand your bullies. Start thinking like a detective!

1. Has it ever occurred to you that your bullies may be targets of bullying themselves? Write down your answer plus any thoughts that you have:

Comment: Studies have shown that many bullies are targets themselves. Consequently, it is possible that your bully is bullying you because they are being bullied themselves. Although this does not solve your problem, it may make it easier on you to realize that you are not alone and that the bullies may not have anything against you personally. You may be part of a bigger picture.

Advice: Watch and listen carefully to see if your bully is being picked on by others.

2. Pick out a person from your bullies' group who seems the least aggressive and intimidating. Watch him or her carefully. Try to see if you have any interests in common. For example, you may find out that you like the same bands, sports teams, magazines, TV shows, movies, or activities.

Write down your answer plus any further observations that you have:

Comment: Finding common interests with your bully/bullies is a good way of making the bullies see you as more than just a target. Also, it's a good way for you to see the bullies' human qualities, which will make them seem a lot less intimidating.

SURVIVING BULLIES WORKBOOK

Advice: Because bullies are human, the more you discover about a bully, the more likely you are to find that you have some interests in common with him or her. If you do find common interests, spend some time thinking about how you can introduce a common interest subject into conversations. At a later date, make an effort to talk to the bully (in a friendly way) and try to introduce a subject that you think the bully likes into your conversation. We are not recommending that you try and join the bullies' group. We ARE recommending that by finding common interests with some members of the bullies' group, you can reduce the group's hostility and judgments against you.

3. Are any of the bullies friends with someone who you are friends with (or someone who you feel comfortable around)?

Write down your answer and any additional observations:

Comment: Sometimes a friend of your parents may know the bullies' parents, or a brother or sister of your friend may know a sibling of the bully.

Advice: Ask your friends if they know of any connections with the bully or his/her family. You may be able to find out what the bullies' "hot buttons" are. For example, if a bully is known to support the Boston Red Sox, it may be wise not to bring up the New York Yankees in conversation. The more you know about your bullies' likes and dislikes, the more skilled you will become at handling them.

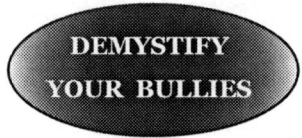

4. Everyone, including bullies, are afraid of certain things. When you think hard about your bullies, can you guess what each one of them may be afraid of?

Write down your best guesses:

Comment: Being afraid of bullies is quite normal. Dealing well with your personal fears, what you could call your "Fear Monster," is a big challenge. The art is to learn how to appear calm in front of the bullies because, unfortunately, the more afraid you appear, the more likely the bullies are to torment you.

Advice: Being afraid is healthy (it is a protection system that makes you careful, cautious, alert and ready to run away). Learning how to manage fear takes time and is a skill to be learned. With practice, you can improve your handling of your "Fear Monster" substantially. Observe the bullies carefully. You will see that they may be afraid, too - afraid of getting caught bullying you, afraid of losing face in front of their classmates, afraid of being bullied themselves, etc.

5. Where do the bullies usually hang out? Have you carefully worked out routes around the school that you could start taking that might reduce the chances of you bumping into the bullies?

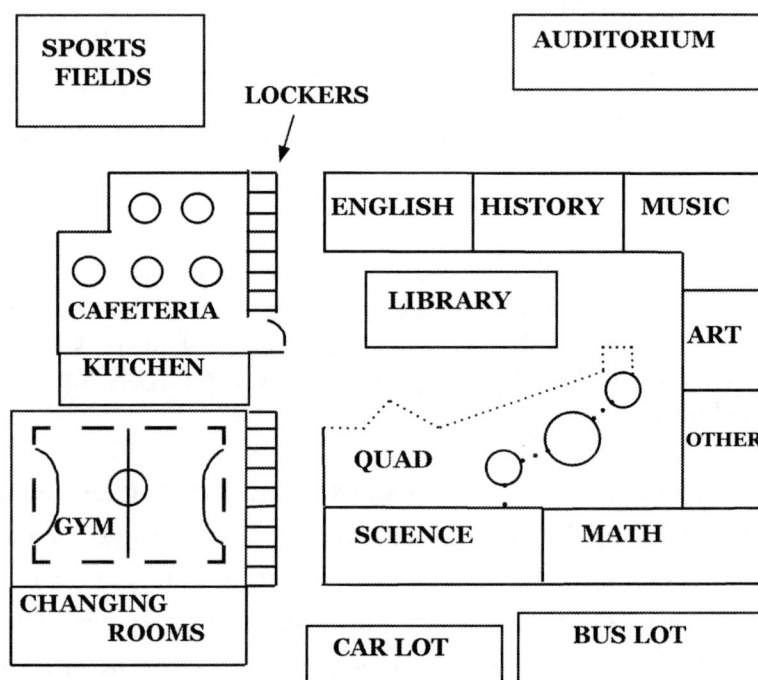

SPORTS
FIELDS

AUDITORIUM

LOCKERS

ENGLISH | HISTORY | MUSIC

LIBRARY

ART

CAFETERIA

KITCHEN

OTHER

QUAD

GYM

SCIENCE | MATH

CHANGING
ROOMS

CAR LOT

BUS LOT

Advice: Bullies often have favorite places at certain times of the day where they like to hang out or cruise about. See if you can watch the bullies and identify their favorite hang out places and cruising zones. Then draw a map of your own school like the one above and mark in the "Bully Areas" on your map. Then work out a "Bully Area" avoidance plan (i.e. maybe you could walk a different way to class, or go early to a particular class, etc.). There is an old saying, "Out of sight, out of mind." The less the bullies have contact with you, the less likely they are to pick on you.

SURVIVING BULLIES WORKBOOK

ACTION: UNDERSTANDING YOUR BULLIES

Directions: Go through the actions listed below. Determine when you can complete each action and circle "Now" or "Soon." Once you've completed an action, come back to this page and put a check mark in the box next to the action. Think about how good it will feel once you've checked off all the boxes. The mission continues!

	Circle One	Done
1. When are you going to find out if your bullies are being bullied themselves?	Now Soon	☐
2. When are you going to observe and figure out what interests you have in common with your bullies?	Now Soon	☐
3. When are you going to find out who your bullies want to impress and get along with?	Now Soon	☐
4. When are you going to find out if any of your friends or family know anything about the bullies or their families?	Now Soon	☐
5. When are you going to find out what your bullies are afraid of?	Now Soon	☐
6. When are you going to draw a map of your school and mark on it where the bullies hang out and at what time they like to cruise certain areas?	Now Soon	☐

*List below any other ACTION STEPS that you can think of that will help you better understand the individuals who are bullying you.

1.

2.

3.

4.

Time for some demystifying.

Yep! Let's DO it!

Mommy! I want my blankie!

CONGRATULATIONS!

You've successfully completed this challenging mission:

"DEMYSTIFYING YOUR BULLIES"

TAKE A BREAK AND RECHARGE BEFORE YOUR NEXT MISSION!

Cheers,
Your Mission Control Team

P.S. We gave you difficult tasks on this mission. Don't feel discouraged if some tasks don't go exactly as planned. Congratulate yourself for having found the courage to attempt these tasks! Being bullied is a tough experience to go through. There are no easy answers. The success of this mission is not measured by how well you did at each task, it is measured by how much you've learned from each task.

SURVIVING BULLIES WORKBOOK

MISSION THREE:

ESCAPE FROM THE ISOLATION TRAP!

SURVIVING BULLIES WORKBOOK

ISOLATION TRAP

Here's the way out...

Being bullied pushes an individual out of their circle of friends and away from their classmates. This can be very traumatic for most people because we are all naturally social beings. Friends are important to us, and we all seek to be valued by them. That is why feelings of social rejection caused by being bullied can significantly damage your self-esteem and confidence. Bullied individuals report that rejection makes them feel self-conscious and inferior to others.

One's natural reaction to feeling rejected by classmates is to become reserved and increasingly withdrawn. Unfortunately, damaged self-esteem and declining confidence combined with becoming withdrawn around classmates pushes you down a slippery slope. At the bottom of this slope lies the **Isolation Trap.**

The greatest danger of the Isolation Trap is that you start to pick on yourself. You start to believe, incorrectly, that there is something truly wrong with you. Why else would people pick on you? Being bullied repeatedly creates a distorted sense of reality. You start to convince yourself that your friends and classmates do not like you. What's worse, you may feel as if you are unworthy of their friendship and as if you deserve to be isolated, alone, and picked on. This feeling makes you unapproachable to friends and classmates. Pretty soon, you are knee-deep in the Isolation Trap. You no longer need a bully to make you feel bad. You start to do a pretty good job of it yourself. With every criticism you inflict upon yourself, you bury yourself deeper into the confines of the Isolation Trap.

The Isolation Trap is bad news, especially when you first realize you're trapped in it. We commend you for facing it head on. The good news is: **there is a way out.** The way out is to restore your confidence.

This mission is a series of exercises designed to help you free yourself from the Isolation Trap. In this section, you must climb the "confidence ladder." Successfully climbing up the "confidence ladder" will prep you for your final mission: making friends and allies. This challenge of climbing out of the Isolation Trap will require courage and dedication, but don't worry. This mission will guide you rung by rung. You're not alone. The mission continues!

SURVIVING BULLIES WORKBOOK

ISOLATION TRAP

Step 1: MOOD CHART

Please fill in the Mood Chart below. Imagine a typical weekday (Monday to Friday), starting from when you first wake up to the hour before bedtime. On a scale from 1-5, "1" being that you feel very gloomy and "5" being that you feel great about yourself, mark in a score for each two-hour window on the Mood Chart. Feel free to add your own comments.

YOUR MOOD CHART

Time	Score (1-5)	Comments
6 am - 8 am		
8 am - 10 am		
10 am - 12 pm		
12 pm - 2 pm		
2 pm - 4 pm		
4 pm - 6 pm		
6 pm - 8 pm		
8 pm - 10 pm		
10 pm - 12 am		

Please continue to the next page.

ABOUT THE RESULTS:

1. Look over the Mood Chart that you filled in. Are you at all surprised by the results? Write down your answer and any thoughts that you have.

Comment: Many people are surprised because they notice that their mood changes at different points in the day. They are also surprised to learn that there are patterns to their mood.

Advice: What you need to do now is look and see when your mood is at its most positive. Then, try to figure out what causes you to feel good at this period during the day. Your goal is to expand this "island of optimism" so that it covers more of your day.

Remember, expanding the "island of optimism" is not an easy task, but it is crucial for you to work on because to climb out of the Isolation Trap, you must:

    1. Stop dwelling on the negative things in your life.

    2. Make yourself concentrate on the positive things in your life.

2. What factors make you feel bad about yourself? Are there certain factors that you can change to improve your mood and self-confidence? Write down your answer plus any thoughts that you have:

Comment: Many factors bring on negative feelings about yourself. Some of these factors such as hormones are outside of your control, but there are two very important factors - sleep and eating habits - that you *can* and *should* control. Sleep is often underestimated in its importance by people of all ages, especially by young adults. If you don't get enough sleep on a consistent basis, your memory, speed of learning, quality of decision-making, emotional balance, and health are all negatively impacted. It is imperative that you get enough sleep, especially if you're being bullied. The stress of being bullied can cause difficulty sleeping. If you're already living a sleep-deprived life, losing even more sleep due to the stress of being bullied can lead to a breakdown of your self-confidence and self-esteem.

Advice on Sleep: Please pay serious attention to the amount of sleep that you're getting. Realistically, you need nine hours of quality sleep for every 24 hours. If your current lifestyle makes it tough to get nine hours of straight sleep at night, make sure you take power naps (30 min - 60 min, but not longer) after school. Interestingly, Winston Churchill, a famous leader during World War II, protected himself from enormous stress by taking power naps whenever he was tired and overwhelmed.

Advice on Eating Habits: Poor food habits lead to glucose crashes. The body, like the fuel tank on a car, only carries a limited reserve of immediate energy (glucose). Going through a glucose crash is like your family's car running out of gas on the highway - a real pain in the neck. Signs of glucose crashes include crankiness, difficulty concentrating, lack of energy, etc. A glucose crash on top of the stress of being bullied is like letting yourself be kicked when you are down. If you're being bullied, don't make your life worse by skipping meals and eating junk food. Eat more fresh fruits, vegetables, wheat bread (a source of good carbohydrates that keeps your energy up), lean meat or fish, and drink lots of water.

The Bottom Line: Being bullied is really tough. Preserve your emotional well-being and strengthen your resilience by making sure that you get enough sleep, good food and make a huge effort not to skip meals.

SURVIVING BULLIES WORKBOOK

Step 2: CONFIDENCE-BUILDING ACTIVITIES

As the Mood Chart highlights, climbing out of the Isolation Trap requires you to stop dwelling on the negative and start concentrating on the positive. To help you develop a pattern of thinking positively about yourself, the next step of the "confidence ladder" works on reminding you of the activities that you enjoy doing or that you are good at. Your goal is to build your confidence by spending more time on these positive activities. Take a look at the list below and check off all the activities that you enjoy doing.

YOUR FAVORITE THINGS TO DO:

Art	Going to the Beach	Singing
Basketball	Karate	Skateboarding
Baseball	Kickboxing	Sketching
Ballet	Hunting	Skiing
Baking	Lacrosse	Snowboarding
Camping	Listening to Music	Soccer
Ceramics	Painting	Squash
Composing	Playing an instrument	Swimming
Cooking	Playing video games	Telling Jokes
Dancing	Reading	Tennis
Debating	Running	Volunteering
Drawing	Sewing	Watching Movies
Fishing	Shopping	Writing

Jot down any other activities that are important to you...

_____

_____

_____

_____

Turn to the next page for advice on how you can use activities to rebuild your confidence.

1. What can I do to re-build my confidence and self-esteem?

Advice: Look at the activities that you have checked. Is it possible for you to spend more time doing your chosen activities? Hopefully it is, because spending time focusing on what you enjoy and/or are good at builds your confidence and bolsters your self-esteem. The better you feel about yourself, the more resilient you are against the negative effects of being bullied.

Comment: Interestingly, high-ranking professional athletes talk about the importance of learning to recover from the self-esteem damage inflicted by losing streaks. Being bullied is like a particularly ugly losing streak in professional sports, only you always have to play again the next day! Like professional athletes, you must teach yourself to get over the damage in self-esteem that comes from losing a string of big games.

2. Don't I risk failure if I take on a new activity when I am feeling down about myself?

Comment: Many individuals caught in the Isolation Trap find it hard to muster the courage to experiment with new activities. You need to remember that it's not your fault that you fell into the Isolation Trap. You got pushed in. Unfortunately, the only person who can get you out of the trap is you. Exploring new activities helps you get over the past and proves to you that you can undertake new adventures and succeed!

Advice: Find the courage to take on a new activity. It will stimulate you, but be careful. When you're emotionally down, taking on a new activity feels more risky than it really is. The uncertainty surrounding the challenges of a new activity can make you excessively self-critical, so much so that you may give up trying the new activity far too soon. Knowing this, when you take on a new activity, be kind to yourself. Work hard to tone down that inner critical voice. Overcoming challenges, step by step, builds deep and lasting confidence. Look back on the previous page. Pick out a new activity and just do it!

SURVIVING BULLIES WORKBOOK

Step 3: AWESOME PERSONAL ATTRIBUTES

When you've been a constant target of bullying, it's easy to forget the great personal attributes that you have. Please take the time to write down five awesome personal attributes that you have in the space provided below. Remember, because thinking positively about yourself is very difficult when you are feeling down, this exercise is an **absolute requirement**. It *will* help you successfully complete your mission of rebuilding your confidence and self-esteem.

Example of five awesome attributes:

1. I have quick reflexes.
2. I am polite to people in stores.
3. I love nature and protect the environment.
4. I know a lot about late 70's punk rock.
5. I am kind to old people.

*ABSOLUTE REQUIREMENT: Write down five of your "Awesome Personal Attributes" (ask your friends or family for help if you're stuck).

1._____

2._____

3._____

4._____

5._____

*DO *NOT* GO ONTO THE PAGE UNTIL YOU HAVE COMPLETED THIS EXERCISE!

Step 4: YOUR PERSONAL BUSINESS CARD

Now, it's time to create your personal business card using your "Awesome Personal Attributes." Check out the example below. Then turn to the next page to start creating your own business card!

EXAMPLE: MY PRIVATE BUSINESS CARD

Front:

Surviving Bullies Inc.

Mr. Colby Eans
Writer

Email: coolbeans@thisisanexample.com

Back:

Best Qualities:

Courageous
Kind
Smart
Hard working
Musical

Step 4: YOUR PERSONAL BUSINESS CARD (cont.)

Get ready to create your very own personal business card! This business card is a concise way of presenting your best qualities and strengths to yourself. Remember, like all of this workbook, your personal business card is private and confidential. It has been created to remind you of your "Awesome Personal Attributes," especially when you are feeling down. Follow the directions provided below.

Fill in the blanks according to the directions provided. Then cut along the dotted line. Paste the sides back to back to create your personal business card.

Front:

a._____

b. _____

c. _____

Email:_____

Back:

Best Qualities

_____
_____
_____
_____
_____

DIRECTIONS:

a = Company Name
Be creative!

b = Your Name

c = Job Title
Activity you're good at.
(e.g. swimmer, writer, musician, comedian, etc.)

Best Qualities:
List the top five traits from "Awesome Personal Attributes" section

Note: This is your personal business card, be careful not to lose it!

SURVIVING BULLIES WORKBOOK

ISOLATION TRAP

Step 5: TAKE THE PLEDGE

TAKE THE PLEDGE:

1. I pledge to place my personal business card in a private and safe place (e.g. inside the drawer of your bedside table).
2. I pledge to read the contents of my personal business card at the beginning of my day and at the end of my day.
3. I pledge to sleep more and to take power naps when I am stressed and tired.
4. I pledge to eat healthy food and not skip meals.
5. I pledge to stop dwelling on the negative things in my life.
6. I pledge to make myself concentrate on the positive things in my life.

Signature: _____

SURVIVING BULLIES WORKBOOK

Step 6: EXPERIMENT

When you are knee-deep in the Isolation Trap, one of your toughest challenges is having the courage and confidence to make new friends. As the "Awesome Personal Attributes" section demonstrates, you possess wonderful personal attributes. Although it may be hard for you to imagine, these are the very qualities that potential friends are looking for. To help you get better at making friends, conduct the following simple experiment and record your results.

EXPERIMENT:

Carefully pick out a friendly individual at your school who you do not know well. When an opportunity arises (i.e. when you walk past them in the halls or if you walk past their desk before class starts or if you're waiting in line to get lunch, etc.), look the person straight in the eyes, raise your hand in greeting and/or say "Hi" in a friendly manner. Walk away naturally.

RECORD YOUR RESULTS:

QUESTION	COMMENTS
1. What exactly did I do?	
2. What was their response?	
3. What do I feel was their reaction?	

Please continue to the next page.

SURVIVING BULLIES WORKBOOK

ISOLATION TRAP

Step 6: EXPERIMENTAL RESULTS

ABOUT THE RESULTS...

Once you have conducted the experiment, your answer to Question No.1 should record, *"I raised my hand, said 'Hi' and walked on."* Your answer to Question No.2 should record that the individual, *"Smiled and said 'Hi' back"*, (if the individual did not see your greeting, or ignored you - do the experiment again). Your answer to Question No.3 could be, either, *"they smiled because they think I am a dork,"* or, *"they smiled because they like me."* The million dollar question is: how accurate is your response - have your feelings of self doubt negatively distorted your answer to Question No. 3?

At this point you may be asking, what is this experiment all about? The answer is simple. Individuals who are caught in the Isolation Trap talk about a big problem of distorting reality when it comes to first meeting people. They admit that they often expect hostility and unfair criticisms from strangers and acquaintances alike. The reality is: *If the strangers and acquaintances are questioned afterwards, they are most likely to report having absolutely no negative feelings toward the bullied individual!* Interesting! The crucial point is that individuals who are caught in the Isolation Trap have a tendency to expect hostility and unfair criticism from others. The reality is, however, others actually harbor no negative feelings towards them! Try this simple experiment for yourself several times. Remember, it is just an experiment, you have little to lose and a lot to gain. Good luck!

CONGRATULATIONS!

We are OUTTA here!

You've successfully completed this

challenging mission:

"ESCAPING FROM THE ISOLATION

TRAP"

GET A GOOD NIGHT'S SLEEP
AND RECHARGE BEFORE YOUR NEXT MISSION!
(You've earned it!)

Cheers,
Your Mission Control Team

P.S. We gave you many difficult tasks and questions on this mission. Don't feel discouraged if any of these tasks don't go as planned. Congratulate yourself for having found the courage to attempt these tasks. Being bullied is a tough experience to go through. There are no easy answers. Remember, the success of this mission is not measured by how well you did at each task, it is measured by how much you've learned from it.

SURVIVING BULLIES WORKBOOK

MISSION FOUR:

DEVELOP YOUR BULLY ANTIDOTE

SURVIVING BULLIES WORKBOOK

Developing Your Bully Antidote...

Congratulations on climbing out of the Isolation Trap! It's now time to develop your bully antidote!

Many individuals who have been caught in the Isolation Trap describe a feeling of being paralyzed emotionally - overwhelmed by the negative criticisms and threats from the bullies - as if they had been poisoned. Ultimately, the emotional impact of being bullied is a lot like being poisoned.

Many individuals who are targets of bullying believe that the reason they are being bullied is because there is something wrong with them. *Please do not fall into this way of thinking.* There is absolutely nothing wrong with you. You just need to develop your own personalized bully antidote booster shot.

Bullies tend to target individuals who possess different qualities than their own. The qualities that make you different from the bullies could be the way you dress, the way you speak or just the fact that you like rock music while the bullies and their friends like hip-hop. The issue is not whether your qualities are good or bad, but that they differ from the average of the bullies' group.

For example, it is quite common for the best-looking girl in her class to get bullied. This may seem surprising to you, but the bullies are actually picking on her for the same reasons that they pick on you. They single her out because her looks make her different from the group.

Please continue to the next page.

Developing Your Bully Antidote...(continued)

On the "Develop Your Bully Antidote" mission, you are going to see yourself from the bullies' perspective. Try to work out how the bullies might see you as different from themselves. Particularly, you need to figure out how the bullies may see you as unusual in terms of your appearance, your interactive style, and your general knowledge.

You are probably thinking at this point, "Does it really matter how the bullies see me?" The answer is strongly: YES, IT DOES.

Once you understand how the bullies see you, you can understand why they are picking on you. As soon as you know why you are a target, you can begin to prepare your bully antidote formula to boost your "bully immune system" - the same way your doctor would give you a booster shot to protect you from chickenpox.

The "Develop Your Bully Antidote" mission consists of personal questions that you need to answer openly and honestly. The questions are designed to help you think through possible reasons why the bullies are targeting you. You will also get practical tips on how to make yourself less of a target.

Remember, when you answer the questions, do not think in terms of good or bad qualities. Instead, try to pretend that you are a highly paid specialist hired to figure out the best way to strengthen your social defenses against being bullied.

Go ahead and try to look at yourself through the bullies' eyes!

SURVIVING BULLIES WORKBOOK

Appearance

How you appear to your bullies is important. The clothes you wear, your hairstyle, skin color, weight, fitness level, etc., all fall under the category of your appearance. To create a powerful bully antidote, you need to think through how you can neutralize certain aspects of your appearance that may be waving red flags at the bullies.

1. Does the clothing you wear look much different from the fashion trends of your classmates?

Write down your answer plus any further observations that you have:

Comment: This is not an easy question because it requires you to closely observe the fashion styles that are popular among your classmates and then compare their styles to your own.

Advice: Bullies often target individuals who stand out from the group. For example, if you are a girl, it may be that you like to wear expensive jewelry. This is great for individual expression, but it could be that your handsome jewelry is making you stand out from your classmates and acting as a red flag to the bullies. Consequently, you might consider wearing modest jewelry for a few months and seeing if this tactic lets you "blend into to the crowd" making you less visible to the bullies.

Please continue to the next page.

SURVIVING BULLIES WORKBOOK

BULLY ANTIDOTE

Appearance

2. Please review the following specific clothing style questions and answer yes or no to each question.

	Circle One
a. Do the high-heels, sneakers, or flip-flops, etc. you wear match the styles worn by your classmates?	Yes No
b. Do the pants, skirts or dresses you wear match those of your classmates?	Yes No
c. Do you wear unusual shirts, sweaters, coats or hats that make you stand out from your classmates?	Yes No
d. Do you wear jewelry that is much different from your classmates'?	Yes No
e. Do you have an unusual hairstyle or have you colored your hair in a special way recently?	Yes No
f. Do you wear very expensive clothes that others in your class might not be able to afford?	Yes No
g. Do you wear secondhand clothes that perhaps belonged to a brother or sister that look out of fashion when compared with your classmates' clothes?	Yes No

Comment: Study your classmates' clothing styles carefully and make sure you have answered the yes and no questions accurately.

Advice: Ask yourself, "Is my clothing style making me stand out from my classmates?" If your answer is "yes," then ask yourself the next question, "Is my clothing style acting as a 'red flag' to the bullies?" If you answer "yes" again, then consider modifying your clothing style so that it blends in more with your classmates'. Try using this blending-in tactic for a few months and see if it makes you less of a target. Remember, this is not changing your individuality. You know the clothing style you like. You are just being tactical and trying to neutralize your appearance.

Appearance

3. Are you prettier or more handsome than the average individual in your school, or are you an outstanding athlete or student?

Write down your answer plus any further observations that you have:

Comment: Individuals who are naturally very good at things, or who are born with great athletic talent or who have especially handsome looks stand out from the group. Some individuals become jealous of people who have special talents, and this jealousy or rivalry can lead to bullying.

Advice: If you are fortunate to be especially gifted in some way but are getting bullied, be careful how you handle the presentation of your special qualities to your classmates. For example, if you are a strikingly good-looking girl and are getting picked on, work on comments that downplay your good looks. If you are a great athlete, and you are getting cruel comments behind your back, be careful not to praise yourself too much around your classmates. If you are the super smart kid who is always the first to answer questions in class, and you are being taunted for being the teacher's pet, try sharing a bit of the glory by letting others be the first to raise their hands in class.

4. Are you much taller or shorter, fatter or thinner, or do you look ethnically different compared to the average individuals in your school? Do you feel that you are being picked on because of your differences?

Please continue to the next page.

SURVIVING BULLIES WORKBOOK

Appearance

Write down your answer plus any further observations that you have:

Comment: Being taller, shorter, fatter, thinner, having lighter or darker skin, etc. makes a person different. Embrace these differences because they are what makes you an individual. It's important that you work on feeling proud of who you are, flaws and strengths included. Remember, every one of your classmates has strengths and weaknesses, even though they may seem perfect to you.

Advice: If you are self-conscious about certain qualities in your appearance, try to avoid the trap of thinking too much about them when you are around others. The reality is: the more self-conscious you are because of certain differences, the more bullies sense your vulnerability, and the more they will target these differences. Rather than being overly defensive about what makes you different, try to focus on what you have in common with your classmates. For example, a love of music is a common bond among all individuals regardless of their size, skin color or body type. Look carefully for interests that you share with your classmates and make sure that you bring them up in conversation whenever an opportunity presents itself.

> *Time for a break!*
> *You've completed the "Appearance" portion of this mission.*

SURVIVING BULLIES WORKBOOK

Interactive Style

Interactive style refers to the way an individual behaves around others. Elements such as the pitch of your voice, the way you make eye contact, whether or not you interrupt others in conversation all fall under the category of "interactive style." Becoming aware of your interactive style is important because interactive styles affect the way others think of you and respond to you. Becoming more aware of your interactive style is also important because it could be attracting bullies to you.

1. Because of your shyness, do you mistakenly come across as aloof and/or "stuck up?"

Write down your answer plus any further observations that you have:

Comment: If you are quiet and shy, bullies may confuse your shyness with arrogance. This may be making you a target to the bullies.

Advice: It's a good idea to come up with a few good lines that you could say about yourself to the bullies in passing. For example, you could say, "Sometimes people confuse my quietness with 'stuck-upness,' which is very frustrating to me because I know I am not very good at X (something you are not good at)". Although this sounds hard to do, if you practice some sentences at home in front of your mirror or with a friend, you may be able to gradually help bullies realize that you are just shy and not stuck-up. This would make the bullies less annoyed by you and more likely to leave you alone.

2. Do you crowd others' air space by standing too close to them or do you make them uncomfortable by moving in and out of their air space too suddenly?

Write down your answer plus any further observations that you have:

Comment: Your body language impacts people around you. Be especially aware of the body messages that you send to bullies because you may be accidentally annoying them with your body language. For example, if you are in the habit of standing close to people, you may be accidentally "crowding" their air space. Crowding a person's air space, especially if you do it suddenly, may result in an individual reacting defensively or even with hostility towards you. Equally, if you are in the habit of standing several yards away from people when you are talking to them, they may feel that you do not like them or do not trust them, which may make them uncomfortable around you.

Advice: Try to observe your own body language while you are with others. Check with yourself to see if you do any of the following: 1. Do you smile nervously for minutes on end? (Makes others nervous). 2. Do you frown a lot? (Makes others think you are angry with them). 3. Do you make sudden movements with your hands? (Can alarm and annoy people). 4. Do you crowd people's air space? (Can make people defensive). 5. Do you fold your arms in front of you or do you clench your fists because you are anxious? (Can make people think you have hostile intentions). 7. Do you tend to avoid making eye contact walking down the hall or on the bus? (You may be advertising your lack of confidence). 8. Do you tend to stare at others? (Can make people uncomfortable). The bottom line is, be aware of your body language and make sure you avoid giving signals that make others uncomfortable.

3. If you become nervous or scared or humiliated by bullies, do you become emotional and/or behave aggressively?

Write down your answer plus any further observations that you have:

Comment: Being bullied is humiliating, especially if it happens in front of others. Bullied individuals often report feelings of personal shame when they look back on their bullying incidents. Once you are trapped in a pattern of being continually bullied, not surprisingly, your humiliation and shame grow powerfully, as do your anger and frustration. Reservoirs of deep anger can make you suddenly strike out at your tormentors with savage words or violent physical action. Reservoirs of deep frustration can betray your vulnerability by causing you to lose your "cool" and cry in front of your bullies.

Advice: Bullies are typically more powerful than you, and they usually out-number you. This gives them a totally unfair advantage. Given that you are at such a fundamental power disadvantage, try your best not to let the bullies deliberately provoke you into any form of violently aggressive action because you will probably lose. Not only will you lose, but worse, the bullies will probably increase their aggressiveness towards you and their frequency of attacks on you. Not easy advice to follow, but as best you can, try not to escalate confrontations, especially when you are out-numbered and out-powered. Also, try your best to control any tearful outbursts. When you find yourself on the brink of tears, take several deep breaths and do your best to tune the bullies out. Remember, emotional outbursts provide the bullies a satisfying sense of power and fuel future attacks.

4. Do you tend to get nervous in front of others and consequently screw up punch lines in jokes or stories?

Write down your answer plus any further observations that you have:

Comment: When you are popular with a group, they do not mind if you make mistakes while telling stories or making jokes. This allows you to feel relaxed and free from stress. Unfortunately, being bullied isolates you and pushes you away from your classmates. This places you under stress around them, which makes telling of stories and jokes much harder, as you probably feel like everyone is watching and judging your every move.

Advice: Professional actors and actresses who regularly perform on stage before hundreds of people always practice their lines and jokes repeatedly in front of a mirror at home. It's a good idea for you to practice key story elements and joke punch lines at home before telling them to groups at school, but remember to be kind to yourself. Forgive yourself when you mess up a story or a punch line. Remind yourself that nearly everybody who has experienced the stress of being bullying report that their ability to tell good stories and jokes goes downhill.

5. Do you talk a lot about your achievements and come across as a "big head" who needs to be "put in his or her place"?

Please continue to the next page.

Write down your answer plus any further observations that you have:

Comment: Individuals who praise themselves in front of classmates run the risk of making others jealous or irritated by their "big headedness."

Advice: Bragging about yourself makes you a target to bullies. Be careful about this. If you are one who tends to brag, make an effort to tone it down. Many individuals who find themselves in uncomfortable social situations try to look cool by bragging about themselves. Classmates can easily mistake your attempt to build yourself up for arrogance. Consequently, try to give yourself "pep" talks in private rather than in front of your classmates. In your private "pep" talks, focus on your strengths and remind yourself to stop dwelling on your weaknesses. Remember, boosting your confidence is critical to your interactive style because when you feel confident about yourself, you won't feel the need to brag in front of others.

6. Is your voice unusual in that it is loud, high-pitched, squeaky, whiney or has a strong accent?

Write down your answer plus any further observations that you have:

Comment: Bullies pick on individuals who are different. The pitch of your voice or your accent may be attracting the bullies to you.

Advice: Try to listen to your voice. You could record it on your computer or your home telephone answer machine, so that you can hear how it sounds. If you have a really loud voice, try speaking more quietly. If you have a strong accent, try your best to pronounce words clearly so that others can understand you better. If you have a squeaky voice, try to speak in a slightly lower voice. Remember, you are not trying to alter your individuality. You are just trying to neutralize parts of your style that may be attracting the bullies to you.

7. When others talk about their favorite subjects that you are not familiar with, do you, in attempt to take part in the conversation, have a tendency to say anything that comes into your head?

Write down your answer plus any further observations that you have:

Comment: This is a critical issue to be aware of. You need to be really honest with yourself about this topic because bullies sometimes target people who come across as a "bull-shitter" or a "poser." Keep in mind that people often become friends with one another because they share an area of interest. For example, a group of boys tend to become friends because they like the same sports team. Because they spend so much time watching and talking about the team, they become "experts" on the topic.

Advice: It is important that you avoid the major mistake of trying to gain acceptance to a group of "experts" by *pretending* that you know about a topic as much as they do. If you really want to become a part of the conversations that the "experts" are having, do your homework and become an equal "expert" so that you can win the groups respect rather than irritating them.

8. In your enthusiasm (or anxiety) to be accepted by a group, do you try to "butt" your way into the group's conversations rather than moving in carefully and slowly?

Write down your answer plus any further observations that you have:

Comment: It's always an awful feeling when you find yourself in a group situation where you don't know the people very well, while everybody else seems to be best friends with one another except with you. It's also an unpleasant feeling when you constantly see a group of friends hanging out with one another, while they consistently exclude you from their group. Many individuals in these "outsider" situations feel desperately "uncool," and they make the mistake of "butting" into conversations abruptly in attempt to fit in and mask their "outsider" status. This approach often backfires because it causes awkward moments and draws negative attention to the outsider. Especially if the outsider is not well-versed in the topic of conversation, he or she is likely to make ignorant comments and "look dumb." This will only magnify his or her "outsider" status.

Advice: If you find yourself in situations where you feel like an outsider, it's important to fight the impulse of jumping into the group's conversation. Instead, try to ease your way in. If it's a group of three or more people, stand next to someone who is also listening. Quietly ask that person what the group is talking about without disrupting the ongoing conversation. Make positive comments to that person's responses, and try to strike up a conversation with him or her. If that person is part of the group, your conversation will attract the other members' curiosity, and soon they will join in on your conversation.

Time for a break!
You've completed the "Interactive Style" portion of this mission.

SURVIVING BULLIES WORKBOOK

General Knowledge

General knowledge refers to the knowledge you learn outside of your classes regarding things like movies, TV shows, sports teams, fashion, etc. You acquire general knowledge from watching TV, listening to the radio, reading books and magazines, browsing the web, and just talking to your friends and family. Having a general knowledge base similar to your classmates is important because it gives you topics to talk about with them. Without this common knowledge base, it's often much harder to strike up a conversation with your classmates. In these situations, your silence runs the risk of being misunderstood as "stuck-up" or socially awkward, which can make you a target to the bullies.

1. Are there times when you feel excluded from your classmates because they are talking about "cool" movies or "in" TV shows that you have not seen?

Write down your answer plus any further observations that you have:

Comment: "Coolness" has a dynamic quality. Different groups of individuals have different measures of what is currently "cool" or "uncool." Consequently, understanding what your classmates consider to be "cool" or "in" this month (as opposed to last month or last year) requires constant monitoring and investigative work.

Advice: Continually monitor what your classmates consider to be "cool" movies and "in" TV shows. If a particular TV show is really popular, make sure you watch a couple of episodes (even if you do not like the show) so that you can join the "cool" conversations about the show. Do the same with popular movies. You do not have to watch every popular film, but you want to be able to demonstrate to the group that you are generally up to speed with the latest movies and are able to comment knowledgeably about

Please continue to the next page.

popular actors and actresses. Remember, being able to take part in the "cool" conversations of others bonds you to their group. Bullies like to pick on outsiders. The more you are able to take part in conversations the harder it is for the bullies to isolate you. Also, as you explore these popular TV shows and movies, you may find that you actually enjoy watching some of them, which allows you to develop a genuine bond with some classmates.

2. Do you often find yourself bored by your classmates' choices in music or books?

Write down your answer plus any further observations that you have:

Comment: Having different musical appreciation or preferring different books to your classmates is unique and commendable. However, bullies may feel that your individual musical taste or your fondness for unusual books is weird and warrants their hostility.

Advice: If the bullies are picking on you for having unusual tastes in books and music, try the "smoke screen" defense to camouflage yourself as a target. The "smoke screen" defense requires that you read a few of the books and listen to some songs that are most popular with your classmates. If you do this, the next time books or music come up in conversation, you will be able to talk knowledgeably with your classmates. The "smoke screen" defense is great because it neutralizes the bullies' accusations that you have weird music and book tastes with minimal cost to you (i.e. you can quietly continue reading and listening to your personal favorites without

the bullies knowing about it). Remember, you can apply the anti-bullying "smoke screen" tactic to any area you choose. Just watch and listen to the group, check out why something is popular. Then do some background homework on that popular subject. Finally, choose your moment carefully and gently join the popular conversations with your newly acquired knowledge. You will fit right in!

5. Would your hobbies be described by your friends as not exactly "main-stream"?

Write down your answer plus any further observations that you have:

Comment: Unusual hobbies can make you look weird to the bullies and consequently they will pick on you. Sometimes people think negatively about an unusual hobby because they believe only "dorky" people like that hobby.

Advice: How about trying the "celebrity halo" defense tactic? Go on the internet or go to your local library or just ask around and see if you can find any "cool" celebrities who share your unique hobby. You may be surprised to find that a famous actor or big football player or rap star shares your interest in the hobby. Once you have collected solid evidence of the celebrity support your hobby has, quietly let people know that Miss Gorgeous Movie Star, etc. loves astronomy or whatever your hobby is. You may be surprised what a good anti-bullying defense the "celebrity halo" can be.

THE CHAMELEON'S CLEVER TACTIC

In the jungles of South America, the chameleon protects itself from creatures that want to "bully" it by changing its colors and blending into its surroundings. By doing this, it no longer stands out as a target to its bullies. Yet as soon as the threat of its bullies passes, the chameleon changes back to its true colors.

Creating a personalized bully antidote by skillfully neutralizing your **appearance**, by polishing your **interactive style,** and by strengthening your **general knowledge**, is rather like the clever chameleon changing its color - both of you become "invisible" to your bullies.

Now on to your FINAL and MOST IMPORTANT mission!

SURVIVING BULLIES WORKBOOK

MISSION FIVE:

MAKE FRIENDS!

Making Friends...

Congratulations on bravely climbing out of the Isolation Trap and developing your bully antidote! You must now undertake your most crucial mission, making friends and allies. This is your ultimate mission because, if you can successfully surround yourself with friends and allies, bullies will find it difficult to pick on you.

Before starting the "Make Friends" mission, please keep in mind that it's unrealistic to become close friends with everyone. Most people only have a handful of close friends, but the wise individuals make considerable effort to bond with others around them. This ensures that they belong to a strong social network.

Connecting with your classmates socially (i.e. forming social allies) does not have the emotional power of a close friendship, but it does have the power of warding off the bullies because it sends a powerful signal of team unity to the bullies. For example, if you are able to say "Hi" to a group of classmates when you walk down the school corridors, and they wave or smile back, it sends the message to the bullies that you command a certain level of social power. This makes the bullies think twice before picking on you.

Bonding with your classmates can be as simple as spending time with them chatting about music, or it can be something more concrete like working with them on a sports team or club. The key to building strong social networks is having the courage to go up to classmates who you barely know and strike up a conversation about a topic you all find interesting. Building your social network can be challenging, but this mission and extra tips found on the *Surviving Bullies* website will help you.

Making Friends...(continued)

Close friendships are special, and they require constant emotional effort from both friends. When one of the friends becomes the target of bullying, considerable stress is placed on the friendship. Often best friends fail to realize how destructive this bullying stress can be. Because of this, it is vital that you find the courage to overcome your pride and do your very best to repair any conflicts between you and your close friend(s) regardless of who you believe is at fault for that conflict. If you can repair and maintain your close friendships, you are sending a strong message to the bullies that their attempts at isolating you from your friends have failed. It also sends the message that when they pick on you, they are actually taking on you and your friends.

On this mission, you must constantly tell yourself that bullies want you to be isolated and on your own. When bullies see you with a close friend, or they see you saying "Hi" to one of your allies, you make the bullies anxious about picking on you. The bullies are anxious because every time they see that you have social power, they worry that your friends and allies will team up against them.

The bottom line is that bullies diminish your social power when they pick on you. Your job on this mission is to re-establish your lost social power by surrounding yourself with close friends and by building a strong social network. Here we go!

SURVIVING BULLIES WORKBOOK

Making New Friends and Allies

The next set of questions is designed to give you practical tips on making new friends and allies. It will take some time and effort, but you can do it. Remember, friends and allies are the key to protecting yourself from the bullies.

1. What do you know about the clubs and organizations that are available for you to join at your school or in your community? Write down some that appeal to you.

Comment: Often a good way of meeting new people is to join a club that encourages individuals to work together. Depending on your age and school, these clubs may include drama, singing, art, sports, martial arts, music, debating, etc.

Advice: Consider joining a club that will help you develop a skill that you are not confident about. For example, if you are shy about telling stories or jokes, join a drama club which will help you overcome your shyness. If you feel physically vulnerable, join a martial arts club, which will help build up your physical confidence. These clubs do not have to be at school. Clubs outside of school have the advantage of expanding your social sphere, which will help you feel less overwhelmed by the bullying you are experiencing at school.

2. Do you find it difficult to go up to a stranger and say hello for the first time? If yes, don't worry because you are not alone. "Breaking the ice" for the first time is one of the most difficult social skills to acquire. To get you started, use the space provided on the following page to make a list of successful "ice-breaking" efforts you've made in the past.

Please continue to the next page.

SURVIVING BULLIES WORKBOOK

Making New Friends and Allies
(cont.)

Comment: There is no guaranteed successful way to introduce yourself to new individuals; however, as a general rule, good "ice breakers" bring up subjects that the person is interested in. If you are not sure what someone really likes, play it safe. Bring up topics such as baby animals with girls and sports' greatest moments with boys.

Advice: Consider developing some "ice breaker" ideas that you can put into simple sentences. For example, if you see a girl wearing a cool watch, introduce yourself to her along with a compliment such as, "Cool watch. Where did you get it?" Make sure that you practice your "ice breaker" phrases by saying them out loud to yourself in private. This way, when you use them, they sound natural.

3. Many individuals who are being bullied in front of bystanders imagine that all the bystanders are hostile to them and are supporting the bullies. Have you looked carefully at the bystanders to see which ones seem troubled by what is happening to you? If yes, describe the specific incidents that you can remember.

Comment: Bystanders who have watched others being bullied often later report being embarrassed that they were afraid to step in and do something to stop the bullies.

SURVIVING BULLIES WORKBOOK

Making New Friends and Allies
(cont.)

Advice: Do a mental re-run of an incident when you were bullied. With your eyes still closed, take a few seconds to review your memory of the bystanders' facial expressions. See if you can observe which of the bystanders seem troubled by what was happening to you. It is likely that the individuals who looked bothered by you being bullied are afraid of being bullied themselves. This is important because it means that these bystanders are potential allies for you. In the next days, try to talk to these bystanders. Remember that they may be looking for an ally against the bullies and need your support just as much as you need their support.

4. Do you admire certain individuals because they seem to have the ability to get along well with most other individuals? If yes, provide specific examples.

Comment: Carefully observe the interactive style of individuals who appear to get along well with other people. Particularly, look to see how these individuals use humor and self-mockery (making fun of yourself in front of others) as "social tools." Also notice how intently these emotionally intelligent individuals listen to other people. The truth is that people like individuals who are humourous and who have the ability to poke fun at themselves in front of others. Also, people who are good listeners tend to be popular because they make others feel respected and important when they listen carefully.

Advice: Consider learning some good jokes that you could tell. For starters, type in "jokes" or "humor" on your internet search engine (i.e. Yahoo, Google, etc.) Learn a few of the best jokes that you can find. Also think

carefully about ways that you could make other individuals smile by displaying the quality of self-mockery. Try to compliment other individuals by making a big effort to listen carefully to them. Not only will your listening suggest that you value them, but you will start to understand them better, which will make it easier for you to talk to them in the future.

5. Especially if you are a boy, but for girls as well, have you considered asking an elder girl team captain for some advice about your bullying problem? Write down your answer plus any ideas that you have:

Comment: Girl team captains are often selected by other people because they are respected by them. They are usually good at resolving conflicts and getting others organized. Girl team captains are often quite mature and confident and like to help younger individuals with their problems.

Advice: See if you can identify an elder girl captain who has a reputation for being kind. Find the courage to go up to her and ask her if she could give you some advice about your bullying problem. Tell her that she has a reputation for kindness which is why you have approached her. She will be complimented. Do not pour your heart out on the first occasion as this may be too overwhelming. Just ask her if there would be a time when she might listen to you. Elder girls like being able to help individuals solve emotionally difficult problems. Team captains know many individuals and they may be able to get some of their friends to help you as well. Log on to www.survivingbullies.com to read about Brian's Story.

SURVIVING BULLIES WORKBOOK

MAKE FRIENDS!

Taking Action: Making New Friends

Directions: Go through the actions listed below. Determine when you can complete each action and circle "Now" or "Soon." Once you've completed an action, come back to this page and put a check mark in the box next to the action. Think about how good it will feel once you've checked off all the boxes. The mission continues!

Questions:	Circle One	Done
1. When are you going to begin learning new jokes and humorous stories that you can tell?	Now Soon	☐
2. When are you going to start working on ways that you can poke fun at yourself in public so that other individuals can see that you are approachable?	Now Soon	☐
3. When are you going to start working on improving how carefully you listen to other individuals?	Now Soon	☐
4. When are you going to start working on your empathy skills (i.e. the skill of understanding what other individuals - especially individuals who you do not like - may be thinking)?	Now Soon	☐
5. When are you going to start reaching out to bystanders who seem to disapprove of bullying? (Remember, these individuals are potential allies for you).	Now Soon	☐
6. When are you going to start learning about potential clubs that you could join?	Now Soon	☐

Please continue to the next page.

SURVIVING BULLIES WORKBOOK

MAKE FRIENDS!

Taking Action: Making New Friends

Questions:	Circle One	Done
7. When are you going to start working on your "ice breaker" skills?	Now Soon	☐
8. When are you going to ask an elder girl team captain for some advice about your bullying problem?	Now Soon	☐

*List below any other ACTIONS that could potentially help you build new friendships and strengthen your social networks in your grade, school or community.

    1.

    2.

    3.

    4.

SURVIVING BULLIES WORKBOOK

Repairing Damaged Relationships

When you are being bullied, life gets tough. This is a time when you need to make sure that you patch up old conflicts, soothe jealous interactions and apologize to your existing friends for any poor behavior in the past. To admit that you may have treated a friend badly is hard to do. Apologizing to a friend requires considerable courage. However, if you can overcome your pride and find the courage to apologize to a friend, you will be rewarded by improved self-esteem and increased respect from your friends. The more friends respect you, the more they will try to help you with your bullying problem. The questions in this section are designed to help you to gauge the state of your relationship with existing friends.

1. In the last year, have you behaved badly towards one of your friends? If yes, describe the specific incidents that you can remember.

Comment: All of us, on occasion, behave badly towards our friends. Why we do this is complicated. Sometimes we do unkind things because we are in a bad mood. Sometimes we are sad about events in another part of our life and unfairly take this sadness out on our friends because they are close by. Sometimes we retaliate when our friends hurt our feelings as a kind of "payback." Sometimes we hurt our friends because we have become jealous of their qualities or achievements.

Advice: When you are being bullied, you need all the friends that you can get to support you. If you feel that you have been guilty of treating a friend badly, make an effort to patch-up any unresolved spats. Pride makes it hard to apologize, but you have a great deal to gain and you may be surprised by how much your friends appreciate the apology. They will also respect the courage you demonstrate through making an apology.

Please continue to the next page.

SURVIVING BULLIES WORKBOOK

Repairing Damaged Relationships
(cont.)

2. Have you, in the last year, tried to "steal" a boyfriend or girlfriend away from a friend of yours? If yes, describe the specific incidents that you can remember.

Comment: It is natural to compete with your classmates for girlfriends or boyfriends. Unfortunately, this competition can result in increased levels of jealousy. Jealousy is a powerful emotion that can result in some individuals deciding that they want revenge for their hurt feelings. This desire for revenge can take the form of individuals deciding to gang up against you and bully you.

Advice: Think carefully if any of your actions over the last year may have caused other individuals to become jealous of you. If you can think of some reasons why other individuals may have become jealous of you, carefully consider ways that you could behave in the future that might lessen this jealousy. To help you gauge your friends' reactions, ask yourself how you would feel if your friend(s) had behaved the way you did.

3. Do you criticize your friends more than you praise them? If yes, describe the specific incidents that you can remember.

Please continue to the next page.

SURVIVING BULLIES WORKBOOK

MAKE FRIENDS!

Repairing Damaged Relationships
(cont.)

Comment: Individuals who are being bullied often experience "raw" emotions that are hard to control. Bullied individuals report that the stress of being bullied can make them overly critical of their friends. Too much criticizing of friends tends to push them away from you, which sadly, makes you feel worse and even more stressed out.

Advice: If you have noticed that you are being overly critical of your friends because you are upset about being bullied, make a big effort to do the following three things:

    A. Make a list of the qualities that you like most in your friends.
    B. Be sure to tell your friends how much you like these qualities.
    C. Say positive things to your friends even when you're upset.

4. Can you write down a list of things that your friends especially like doing or talking about? If yes, describe the specific examples.

Comment: Many individuals complain that other people only want to talk about themselves. Boys are often worse than girls in this regard. Emotionally intelligent individuals are often good at bringing up favorite topics of others in conversations. This is a good idea because it makes other people like hanging out and talking to you.

Advice: Make a point of bringing up your friends' favorite topics during your conversations with them, and then make a big effort to listen to them talk. Your friends will be complimented by your interest in them. You will be rewarded by an improvement in your relationship with them.

SURVIVING BULLIES WORKBOOK

Taking Action: Repairing damaged relationships

Directions: Go through the actions listed below. Determine when you can complete each action and circle "Now" or "Soon." Once you've completed an action, come back to this page and put a check mark in the box next to the action. Think about how good it will feel once you've checked off all the boxes. The mission continues!

Questions:	Circle One	Done
1. When do you plan to apologize to a friend whom you may have offended?	Now Soon	☐
2. When are you going to start making sure that you praise your friends more than you criticize them?	Now Soon	☐
3. When are you going to make lists of your friends' favorite topics, hobbies, and interests so that you can bring them up in conversations with them?	Now Soon	☐
4. When are you going to look back on your past actions and figure out if any of them could have caused jealousy from your friends? (Remember, it takes courage to apologize, and it takes wisdom to learn from your mistakes).	Now Soon	☐

*List below any other ACTIONS that you can think of that may help you succeed in repairing damaged relationships that you may have with individuals in your grade, school or community.

1.

2.

3.

4.

CONGRATULATIONS!

**YOU HAVE COMPLETED
THE *SURVIVING BULLIES WORKBOOK!***

Cheers,

Your Mission Control Team

SURVIVING BULLIES WORKBOOK

ABOUT
THE CREATORS

Learn more about:

The Surviving Bullies Project

at www.survivingbullies.com

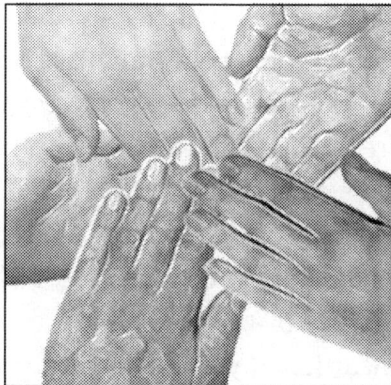

Read on for full Anti-Bullying Agent Profiles and Acknowledgements.

ANTI-BULLYING AGENT: Dickon Pownall-Gray

For three long years, from age 11 to 14, I was cruelly bullied. I was the rich kid from the big house whose parents were TV stars. At first the bullying was name-calling, pushing and shoving, stealing my school bag and filling it with old leaves, etc. About six months into the bullying, I fought back and punched one of the kids from the group who was tormenting me. That afternoon, walking home from school on my own, a small green "Mini" car screeched to a halt next to me. The 17-year-old brother of the boy I had punched jumped out and beat me up. Finally he threw me into a barbed wire fence and drove off laughing. The weight of my body forced the rusty steel barbs so deeply into my flesh that I could not untangle myself from the wire wrapped around me without help. Three agonizing hours later, a kindly lady rescuer was able to slowly pull the barbed wire out of my wounds. Ashamed that the lady could see tears pouring down my cheeks, I turned rudely away and limped painfully into the forest where her kindly cry of, "I will take you home" was muffled by the beech and oak trees. Hidden from my rescuer in the deep forest, I heard, in my head, my father's voice admonishing me, saying repeatedly, "Men don't cry, men don't cry." Deeply humiliated by my inner voice, the "blubbing" got worse. I sank down on top of the leaf-covered ground. Suddenly I began frantically burying myself beneath the newly fallen autumn leaves. Finally completely covered, I lay quite still, buried safely in a warm moldy darkness. To this day my memory is still hazy as to how I got home.

Some time later, at the emergency room, the doctor demanded that I tell him who had done this to me. Knowing that the village boys' honor code absolutely forbade "ratting" on another boy to an adult, I refused to talk. Finally my mother's demands combined with the doctor's orders made me surrender the boy's name. It was the worst decision of my life. The boy was heavily punished. The news quickly spread through the village that I had "ratted". Within a day I was totally shunned by every boy in the village. I was branded the "sneak", the "tattle-tale" – the privileged boy from the big house who now deserved to be beaten up. Three truly awful years followed, in part, because I refused to ever "rat" again. Consequently, I was forced to lie to my parents about each new bruise, split-lip and black-eye. The worst of it was not the physical beatings, but the rejection by my peer group - the intense emotional pain of isolation and the conviction that I deserved what I was getting because I had humiliated my own honor by pathetically "ratting" to an adult.

I am now 51 years old, happily married with three wonderful children. I have written this workbook in the hope that it can help people, both girls and boys, understand why they are being bullied and what specific practical actions they can take to lessen the bullying they are experiencing.

Over the last three years I have listened carefully to young adults telling me their experiences of being bullied. As their stories have unfolded, I have been deeply saddened by the extent of their emotional pain and angered to hear of their humiliations at the hands of others. My listening has made me realize just how difficult it is to be a person coming of age amidst the clatter of the confused moral messages of our American, and increasingly global society. For those of you who talked to me, thank you for your dignity. Thank you for your courage in being so candid. Your contributions have greatly assisted me in writing a workbook that can genuinely help targets of bullying.

I want to express to every bullied young adult who reads this workbook that I know how you feel. I understand how difficult things may be for you at this moment. You are not alone. Believe in yourself no matter what others say. Work hard at the solutions recommended in this workbook and you can make your situation better through your own efforts.

If, after working through this workbook, you feel that you can improve it, please email your suggestions to dickon@survivingbullies.com. I will try to incorporate your new practical ideas into a second edition of this workbook.

Sincerely,

Dickon

ANTI-BULLYING AGENT: Shan Shan Jiang

After moving to the U.S. at nine years old from China, I stopped fitting in. I was one of four Asian kids in a mostly Italian-American school, and that made my life hell. Seventh grade was the worst. Besides the ominous and inescapable "ching chang chung" that people usually utter as they passed me, the chink, in the halls, there were also girls who routinely stuck clumps of tape in my hair on the bus and watched as I struggled to get them out. Their laughters proved that my struggles were mere entertainment for them. Yet to me, it seemed as if they, like leeches, fed upon my misery. It energized them as they consumed all of my self worth, confidence, and any hope for acceptance. Seventh grade was when I experienced loneliness from hell. I felt condemned to perpetual inferiority because the society I knew labeled me as nothing else but a chink and a nerd. And after awhile, everywhere I went, I felt like a thorn, awkward, repulsive, and chinky. It became inescapable, but not because of outside torments. Instead, it was because of my own self-loathing. I began to see myself as a disgusting person, deserving of torment. I hated everything that I was, and, most of all, I hated the irrevocable fact that I was Chinese. Truly, I wanted to die.

Perhaps the only reason why I didn't die was because I found refuge in learning academically and artistically. Slowly, as I focused my attention away from the torments based solely on my heritage, I was able to discover myself, my passions, and my happiness.

I am now 22 years old and a much happier person. I graduated from Yale University in May of 2005 where I studied sociology. I plan to attend medical school in the fall of 2006. I joined Dickon in creating the *Surviving Bullies Workbook* during the second half of the project. From listening to the stories - painful and humiliating in their own way - I am constantly reminded of how profound and thoughtful young adults can be. I seem to have forgotten this fact somewhere along my way to adulthood. Also, I have been constantly inspired by Dickon's compassionate determination to offer practical tools aimed at helping others to understand their own experience and regain control of their situation.

My contributions to the workbook have been driven by reflections of my own experiences combined with a strong desire to help bullied young adults avoid the depths of sadness and isolation that I experienced. I've been there, and I think the advice Dickon and I have poured into the workbook would have made my life a lot less hellish.

If you want to help with a second edition of this workbook, please write down your suggestions and email them to me at: shanshan@survivingbullies.com. Congratulations on completing your missions!

Sincerely,

Shan Shan

SURVIVING BULLIES WORKBOOK

ABOUT THE CREATORS

"Thank You" Missions Contributors

Acknowledgments...

The idea of young adults being bullied upsets people greatly. As a result, for the past three years, the Surviving Bullies Project has been the constant recipient of enormous generosity of spirit from many people. School teachers, parents, medical professionals, librarians, students, have all unselfishly contributed ideas, given candid feedback, and freely donated their most valuable asset, their time.

I want to say thank you to the students of the Eagle Hill School in Hardwick, Massachusetts. Your diligence and your wry humor in filling out the early drafts of the workbook are deeply appreciated. You were always polite with your feedback even when you thought suggestions of mine were "kind of dorky." Thank you, the wonderful teachers at the Eagle Hill School who let me audit their classes. Thank you, Leslie Larrivee, for making it possible to talk one-on-one with many students, and thank you for your thoughtful feedback. A special thank you to Ron Baglio, Assistant Headmaster, the Eagle Hill School. You gave me countless hours from your busy schedule. You spent many hours reviewing drafts. Much more importantly, by watching you with your students, you taught me to be a better father. You showed me with your example, that children will follow and respect a man who continually demonstrates moral integrity, humor, empathy and compassion, yet who leads with firmness and quiet authority.

Thank you Rev. Jennifer Brooks, Minister of the Unitarian Church. Your insights into human nature helped me structure the workbook. Your ideas about the importance of mentors for bullied young adults will be implemented. Thank you Kevin Brooks, for bravely telling me about your bullying experiences. You have handled your difficulties with great courage.

Thank you Jerry Friedman for leading from the front. Your championing of the importance of elder people to our society through your Earth Elders Foundation has been inspirational. You showed me that a man can make an enormous difference in this world if he tries hard enough.

Acknowledgments...(continued)

Thank you Joe Kelly for being a friend who listened as I struggled to understand the "long shadow" of childhood bullying upon my own adult life.

Thank you Shan Shan Jiang for your illustrations, for your emotional honesty, for your insights on bullying, and for your compassion and empathy to those who are being bullied. Your writing contributions, especially your understanding of the ugliness of the Isolation Trap, greatly improved this workbook.

A special thank you to the Surviving Bullies Project academic advisory board. Dr. Golan Shahar, Associate Professor, Behavioral Science Department, Ben Gurion University, you continually inspired me to keep going. Your critical feedback improved the workbook significantly and I forgive you for persuading me to re-write a whole section when I thought I was finished! Dr. Lisa Cross, Assistant Clinical Professor of Psychiatry, Yale University School of Medicine, thank you for explaining to me why young adults are so particularly vulnerable to serious bullying between the ages 11 to 14. Because of you, I now have a deep understanding of how critical this age window is in the development of a person's identity and why being isolated from his or her peer group can seriously harm a young adult's confidence and self-esteem. Dr. Chris Henrich, Assistant Professor, Department of Psychology, Georgia State University, thank you for believing in this project. Thank you for traveling across the USA to give us your advice in person. Your improvements to the Demystify Your Bullies section are greatly appreciated. Your profound understanding of the "inner world" of young adults has helped enormously with the structure of the Surviving Bullies DVD due to be completed next year.

Thank you Lynn Landry from Landry Design Associates (www. landrydesign.com) for the wonderful cover design. I could not have asked for a better design and got much more than I could have hoped for!

Acknowledgments...(continued)

To my wife Lisa, thank you for your constant support, encouragement, and love. To my daughters Alexi, Ella and Saskia, thank you for your great ideas and practical feedback. Mostly thank you for making me laugh; thank you for keeping me young; thank you for being such wonderful fun and for being such sparkling company.

Dickon Pownall-Gray

SURVIVING BULLIES WORKBOOK

ABOUT
THE CREATORS

"Time spent in reconnaissance is seldom wasted."
~ General Pownall

Please visit

WWW.SURVIVINGBULLIES.COM

for further help with bullying problems

ALSO

Please email any practical anti-bullying

solution ideas

that you, your friends or your family have to:

info@survivingbullies.com

Thank you,

DICKON POWNALL-GRAY

SHAN SHAN JIANG

Lightning Source UK Ltd.
Milton Keynes UK
UKOW03f1059200715

255482UK00001B/39/P